Revolution:

A Practical Guide

By:

Kyle Sorenson

ISBN: 9781672476553

Contents:

Section 1-

The Case for Revolution – page 4

Section 2-

How to Revolution – page 27

Section 3-

Rabbit Hole Reads – page 61

About Revolution: A Practical Guide

-The main theme of this book is Liberty and Justice for All.

-This book has only 1 chapter followed by 3 easy steps!

-This book was heavily influenced by George Washington's Farewell Address which is included in the appendix section.

-Yes, I am calling for an actual Revolution.

-Will people be hurt? Perhaps the folks that have corrupted our Democracy should face legal consequences.

-This book is about establishing an Open Source discussion. I don't have all the answers. This is your world. You are a participant. Share your ideas. By writing this book, I'm starting a conversation.

-The Revolution is not televised. It's in your mind.

Section 1

The Case for Revolution

Chapter 1-

The New Patriot Rebellion

Rebellions are built on hope

This literary journey began when I started writing a fictional novel called *The New Patriot Rebellion*. The story is about a group of unlikely heroes who discover a way to dismantle the deep state faction that has infiltrated the United States Government.

These *New Patriots* establish a system that virtually eliminates corruption and truly works toward Liberty and Justice for All.

Inspired by the original U.S. Constitution and the nearly forgotten words of a prominent founding father, the heroes establish a new kind of Open-Source Democracy. One that better fulfills the promise of Liberty and Justice for All. The new system spreads globally and unnecessary suffering is greatly reduced.

While work on the novel continues, I'm publishing this *practical guide* to satisfy a deep sense of urgency within me.

For years I eased my frustrations with injustice and oppression by pondering what a fair government and social system might look like. I even allowed myself to question whether people needed a government at all.

This has been an enlightening quest that has brought me to this space and time… with loads of notes.

Throughout the journey, the ideas that came to me were written out on notebook pages and post-it notes that piled up all over my house. Collectively, these notes paint a picture of how a system could be set up that was accessible, fair, and most importantly *unhackable*.

I suspect this book will be an ever-evolving work like Carla Emery's *An Old-Fashioned Recipe Book* and *Encyclopedia of Country Living*. A living work where each edition contains corrections, elaborations, and additions as new information becomes available.

My ultimate goal is more than promoting *my* ideas, it's about establishing a framework where ideas can be shared freely and the best ideas are illuminated. My motivation is simple. I believe that Peace on Earth is our ultimate goal as a human society. A goal like 'the end of suffering' is obtainable but not if we fail to meaningfully seek it.

In this book I outline a framework where ideas and solutions can be shared without being manipulated or tampered with. I do not have all the answers. The truth is that we each hold small pieces of the answers.

When our individual experiences and perspectives can be shared freely, we will find solutions that would be impossible for any one of us to discover on our own.

It just feels like the time is right for a Revolution, so let's get started!

A Time for Change.

Understanding how something works allows you to properly work with it. In this case, let's understand how change works on a fundamental level.

There is only one moment where change can occur and that moment is NOW. Now is the only time an action like change can take place. Actions can never take place in the past or in the future. Now is the only time we can truly operate in.

You don't decide to lose 30 lbs. and immediately lose the weight. But you *decide to* at this moment. And when you decide to do something now, and again in the next "now", and the next "now", you are constantly moving toward your goal. The process eventually becomes unconscious.

This fact of life is sometimes called the law of attraction. Once you've set your mind to something, you unconsciously attract opportunities that work to fulfill it.

If I have my mind set on Thanksgiving dinner, I can walk through the grocery store and certain items will stand out. Whatever I knowingly or unknowingly associate with Thanksgiving dinner will stand out from the rest of the items. My mind is set on Thanksgiving dinner but what stands out is potatoes, squash, turkey, etc.

If I'm trying to lose weight I may make 100's of small, unconscious decisions throughout a day that work to fulfill my goal. I will recognize opportunities that would have gone unnoticed if I had not decided to make a change.

There are varying levels of this type of focus and the corresponding results are predictable. The more focused a person is from moment to moment, the more effectively they reach the desired outcome.

An athlete might call it "getting in the zone". Harry Potter fans might recognize it as a real-life *Felix Felicis* effect.

You can't do anything in the past or future so operating in the now is the only way to effectively make change. And change is what we need so let's get this Revolution started!

First, let's take a look at where we are at. We are going to have to be painfully honest with ourselves. We are going to have to leave old assumptions behind. This may get uncomfortable but Revolutions are hard so buckle up.

Although it *feels* like things have gotten worse in the world, the reality is that many people have a higher standard of living than ever before. More folks have access to vast amounts of information so there is real progress being made.

There is a small group, however, that might disagree. We are going to call this group **"The Faction".**

For those born into multi-generational power positions, the spread of democracy and systematic freedoms is an encroachment on their position. Their names and numbers change but the system they use to maintain their power remains the same.

Since The Faction have been making the rules, the process has been slow for the rest of us, but we have been making progress.

Voting is arguably the most power we each have and nearly all men and women have secured the right to vote in the U.S. That wasn't always the case, and it was a hard fight.

It is easy to imagine that
The Faction was not thrilled that
more people would have voting
rights. They fought against that
progress and we could assume
that they might still work to
maintain their positions of
power today.

Except we don't have to
assume.

The Faction works to limit
any erosion of their power in
broad daylight. They work
against equality, individual
Liberty, and Justice. They use
propaganda, psychological
warfare, and intimidation to
divide us.

If the population was
informed by facts and data, and

then voted accordingly, it would be the end of The Faction's power.

Power and greed has sickened The Faction to the point that they lack a sense of fairness and moral values. They have no remorse for the injustice they perpetuate in the name of maintaining their power.

Simply put, they are sick. We can't just ask them to "get better", we have to help them. Power corrupts by its very nature. Power seeks more power and the ancient illness takes hold.

The only way for a society to reach the goal of Liberty and

Justice for All is to divide the power evenly. Each citizen holding a small bit within a system that prevents abuse and the concentration of power.

The whole point of the first American Revolution was to wrestle the power from a central force, a king, and establish a system where the power is shared equally. This Revolution will work towards that same end. There is no reason for bloodshed, this is a war of information.

Using the Constitution as a shield and its promises as a sword, we will take a giant leap towards Liberty and Justice for All. Hiiii-yaah!

Fortunately for us, we have some powerful tools to work with. The first tool is recognizing the fact that nothing is more certain to fail than success. Success is blinding. Success rarely allows for correction or adaptation. So as the environment changes over time, the successful mechanisms of yesterday no longer work as well.

A reckless driver who successfully weaves through traffic at a high rate of speed will become more and more emboldened until... the crash. The crash is big and causes a lot of damage because the driver was successful at higher and higher speeds.

This Faction is not tested by consequences. They are rarely challenged. They are rigid and their system will eventually crash. Their system is only artificially held together by teams of lawyers who write their success into legislation that favors their position. They have not had an idea that benefited society for several generations in most cases.

The looming crash will be an opportunity for a new Faction to seize control, so our war must be with *the system* that allows The Faction to exist, not The Faction itself.

This book is a direct result of my many brushes with that system. I've seen, first hand, *the steamy side of the bullshit pile* that works to keep The Faction running things.

Understanding how prolonged success can lead to failure will inspire us to build a better system that has evolutionary flexibility. As new information becomes available and the environment changes, the system adjusts accordingly. The new system must "learn".

The next tool we have is that our struggles have made us skilled warriors. Most of us have survived by being flexible and creative. We have suffered through very uncomfortable times and we have learned a lot along the way. We have marched honorably through unfair circumstances. Navigating the bureaucracy has made us savvy.

Collectively we all have our "life-hacks" to contribute, and when this information is shared freely, we all benefit from the experiences of each other.

The Faction does not have the same experiences. Having power is the only reason they continue to have power. They do not create or do anything meaningful for society. The Faction have crowned themselves kings. They live in the bubble that they have created to protect themselves from interacting with anyone who isn't in their club. When their bubble collapses, they will have no skills to utilize or experience to draw from. Privilege is all they know. They recognize this and will fight fiercely to maintain the system as it is.

We also have sheer numbers on our side. There are a whole lot more of us than those in The Faction. There is also a whole group of folks who might think they are in The Faction but that is an illusion. They are just willing participants who are rewarded with a comfortable lifestyle. We'll call them **"Middle Management".**

These are the politicians, business people, and lawyers who protect and insulate The Faction. The Middle

Management folks see the task of shielding The Faction from any consequences as an honorable career goal. They court favor from The Faction as a measure of security.

The Middle Management are a fierce bunch of problem solvers whose highly developed skills make them a formidable adversary. At a moment's notice, they can round up a posse of lawyers and fight against any challenge to The Faction's power.

If you actually make some sort of dent into their world they will simply hire you or destroy you.

Because they are not actual members of The Faction, Middle Management are not as insulated from moral consequences and reasonably minded influence as The Faction is. We can convert many of them to join our fight. *They are us* after all.

Information is power. With access to the vast amount of shared information on the internet, we each have the power to educate ourselves and create a livelihood that wasn't possible before.

This is perhaps our greatest tool. This is the Achilles heel of The Faction. They cannot control it. It will directly lead to the end of their system.

In this new era of readily accessible information, the citizens are becoming more rounded in their education. They are gaining a more diverse skillset that stands in contrast to the specialization labor of yesteryore. Average folks can learn about a multitude of different vocations and then focus on particular areas of interest.

This is a great improvement over being mindlessly cast into the local factory. This will make the workforce a happier, healthier organization.

Eventually, access to information will spawn a new era of solutions, inventions, and progress. When people have acquired a wide range of knowledge based on what interests them, and outside the narrow channels of academia, they will look at problems from a new, unique perspective.

But first, we must deal with The Faction. Their grip on power is holding us back. Lives could be saved and enriched if only the wheels of progress were allowed to spin freely.

So here we are. The folks in charge are drunk on power and the whole system is headed for a cliff. Sounds rather ominous... we better do something.

I propose we have a Revolution!

Section 2

How To Revolution

How To Guide:

Revolution in 3 easy steps

Revolution in 3 easy steps:

Step 1- Change your mind.

We must question motivations and narratives. Why does someone say this or that? What do they have to gain? Are they blindly repeating something that they heard?

Whether you play the role of the cowboy or the indian, the game is the same. Current U.S. politics is just that, a game of cowboys and indians. Stop playing it, it is all made up. I will repeat this for clarity: IT. IS. ALL. MADE. UP. Reject it all. You are not red or blue and neither is anyone else. So stop playing the game.

We can simply judge ideas by their relationship with Liberty and Justice for All. They will either work towards it or they won't. No need for circle-talking political rambling nonsense.

The Faction and Middle Management use a powerful tool called *controlling the narrative* to keep the conversation on topics that are divisive. They spin narratives that become the talking points of the working-class folks who have been hypnotized into working for The Faction for free. We'll call these folks **"Unpaid Sponsors"**.

This narrative control can be a simple declaration that "You are either with US or against US!" or a bit more nuanced like the loaded question, "Have you stopped beating your wife?" "It's a yes or no question!" they say. But, if you answer "yes" you imply that you were beating your wife and now you have stopped and if you answer "no" then you imply that you are still beating your wife.

You disarm their ability to control you when you reject the premise or narrative. You don't need to have a clear understanding of what the actual narrative might be, just start by rejecting every bit of it.

The Faction tries to convince us that all problems are nails and they are the only ones holding a hammer. We must recognize that the hammer is irrelevant and every problem is not a nail. The whole premise is moot.

Be especially wary of grand claims, they are almost always bullshit sprinkled with a fact or two. There is absolutely no harm in finding a true perspective on a subject.

Are you ready to try this out in real life? Deep breath. No cowboys and indians bullshit. We'll just dive right into a hotbed of controversy to illustrate.

On the topic of abortion rights. Some of us may think we

want abortion to be illegal, but is this really what we want?

Now if we frame the question another way, we may find a solution that most of us can live with and actually get something done. How about, "Would you like to eliminate nearly all abortions?"

I'm going to guess that most of us would answer "Yes, I'd like to eliminate nearly all abortions". Who wouldn't really? I think it would be hard to find anyone who honestly wants to increase the number of abortions. So the question becomes *how to eliminate nearly all abortions.*

Now, a fact that we should recognize is that making things illegal rarely eliminates them.

In fact, try to name one thing that was made illegal and has gone away.

I've asked a lot of really smart people this question and so far no one has come up with anything beyond a few weird chemicals... and lawn darts. This is a very strange situation.

Few people can name a single thing that was made illegal and then went away. Yet the current argument is whether to make abortions go away by making them illegal? It is just plain silly, but it illustrates the point.

The narrative is being controlled for the purpose of division, not for finding an actual solution. There are thousands of things we could do to eliminate nearly all abortions but nothing happens because we are divided with surgical precision.

The Faction needs us to be divided. They could not operate if we were not fiercely divided.

There are many examples of these sorts of manipulations. The best practice is to just throw out the proposed narrative and ask a few questions to establish a direction of action. Don't be an Unpaid Sponsor. We need to stop arguing over false pretenses and get on with the Revolution!

Let experience guide us.

We must take the long view. We must ask where *this or that* is headed? Is there any historical example of where *this or that* is headed? In the case of The Faction and Middle Management, they would have us believe that they've earned their position of power and to change the rules in any way would be "punishing success". And they want you to believe that they can police themselves because they are really honest and smart.

Let the experiences of the past show us the truth! Throughout history, consolidated power and ideas of supremacy have turned out horribly every single time.

We should reject the notion of supremacy of any sort but always reject it within our legal system. You can believe whatever you want personally but you cannot inject any supremacy beliefs into the law.

Our Constitution gives the same rights to everyone. Any notion of supremacy is false and dangerous. History shows us that legalized supremacy turns out to be especially bad.

Our government should protect each individual's Constitutional rights and protect the general population from scammers and cheaters.

Our problem now is that the scammers and cheaters are running the government.

It is Revolution time y'all!

Here is an example of how legal corruption works:

Most would agree that it's wrong for a tire salesman to throw nails out into the road in front of their business. Some might argue that it is smart business, but most would agree that it is shady and should be a crime. So, a large group of tire salesmen simply form a lobbying firm. The lobbying firm gets a law passed making it illegal to punish tire salesman for throwing nails in the road.

This type of legal corruption is happening constantly. And it is important that we stand up to it now.

Free and open market capitalism should not reward through legislative advantage. A good idea is rewarded because it solves a problem or benefits society. Using our legal system to establish an advantage should be a crime and treated the same way we treat any theft.

We can change this. We have to change this.

Instead of making it complicated, we can shrink and simplify the role of government.

All we need to do is ask a few simple questions:

-Does this law or lack thereof promote Liberty and Justice for All?

-Does this situation require regulation?

Rabbit Hole Read! *See Appendix a "Is this Liberty? Is this Justice?"

Revolution in 3 easy steps:

Step 2 – United We Stand, Divided We Fall

We need to establish a trusted information exchange system. Quality decisions are made when there is quality data. That is what we are talking about here, *quality decisions*. Public policies, laws, votes... these are all decisions and we want good ones to be made.

Like any change, big systematic change is not going to happen instantly. But we need to focus on it for it to come at all. That is just how change works.

Liberty and Justice are both moving targets. There is not currently Liberty for all or Justice for all, but there is some Liberty and some Justice. Again, we need to stay focused on these goals or they will never be realized.

What we need is a system that automatically protects the process of gathering quality data and sharing it with the citizens. The citizens can then make quality decisions about who to vote for and the elected officials have a clear understanding of what policies the public wants enacted.

Essentially this will eliminate the effects of shady politics. No more half-truth spewing, slip and fall lawyers being bought up by The Faction!

Quality decisions, quality policies, and the whole system becomes an automatic "Liberty and Justice for All" seeking machine. That would be amazing, but what might it look like?

First, I propose drafting the sports stats research people. This is a war after all! *And I'm only half-kidding*. They can tell you the last time John Madden wiped his ass with his left hand in the southern hemisphere... time, date, latitude, and longitude.

There is no disputing information that is gathered like

game stats. 14 rushing yards is 14 rushing yards... no way to spin it. Is a regulation a good thing or meaningless? Let's compare the data! With the regulation, the data said this, and without the regulation, the data said that. Apples to apples, no spin possible.

Now the entertaining sports announcer guy, he has got all kinds of theories and trending analysis but the stats researcher puts out the raw data and 14 yards is 14 yards. Period.

Before seatbelt laws, x amount of people had broken heads in car wrecks, after seatbelt laws, x amount of people had broken heads. It costs society x amount when someone breaks their head so the savings is <u>x</u>. Is seatbelt use worth being regulated? Let the consensus decide that based on quality data.

Data doesn't lie, it doesn't have an opinion or political affiliation. The only reason not to establish policy this way is if you want to be shady, and boy do The Faction folks want to be shady. They would lose everything if they did not operate in the shadows.

An open and transparent data system would allow any curious citizen to access the data and add their own, sometimes expert, analysis. Why have retired accountants wasting away on golf courses when some would gladly look over the books and make sure nothing shady is going on. They might find possible efficiencies that save public resources.

Citizens policing the government? A freaking great idea! ...unless you're The Faction.

Let's address public debt for a moment.

We badly need a complete and thorough audit of the entire government. Then we can establish a transparent public accounting system.

To think we have a booming economy while adding a trillion dollars to the national debt is lunacy. It's like signing up for 20 credit cards in your grandchildren's name and proudly maxing them all out.

Debt is a method of control and the elimination of excessive public debt is as easy as sitting down with the bills, adding them up, and setting up revenue accordingly. Our public accounting systems can and should be completely transparent. The Faction wants you to believe that this is all way too complicated for you to understand. It is not.

Do you believe that money grows on trees? Well, unless you are a fruit or nut farmer, it does not. Fancy accounting practices are just a tool of thieves.

To recap: we must record data in a simple format like game stats and then allow everyone access to the data so we can compare apples to apples. Only shady intentioned folks will be against this. You'll know 'em when you see 'em. The resistance will be fierce but we must be brave in our quest for Liberty and Justice for All.

*Rabbit Hole Read! *See Appendix b "Dollar Trax"*

Once we have trusted data, we'll need a public venue to analyze, discuss, and come to a consensus on policy.

I propose a social networking type website that is free and open with no advertisements or other financial motivations.

Each citizen goes through an authentication process that is unhackable. This ensures that each participant is exactly who they say they are and they are only represented one time. You might verify your name and address at your post office and receive an activation code that you enter into the system.

Once entered into the system your identity becomes a brick in a block-chain secure data system. Authenticated individuals are then free to share questions, facts, data, opinions, or anything else regarding public policy.

The system then groups similar topics and discussions into weighted forums. The forums are constantly shuffled according to consensus with the most agreed-upon course of action or policy statements ranking first.

It is very difficult to get people to agree on specifics but by watering down an idea until a majority agrees, an initial direction can be established. It is a constantly evolving highway of what I call Dynamic Governance. That is, consensus is free to change at any time... it is dynamic.

New data might change the consensus. A better idea might be discovered. A new technology might be invented. A consensus might be to first gather data that answers a question. Once that question is answered the consensus dictates the next action, and the next.

The power of your vote becomes valuable every day rather than once a year. You can change your mind and support a different consensus at any time. You can stay out of discussions that you have no interest in or knowledge about and participate in discussions that you know or feel strongly about.

This system leaves our Constitution completely in place and works in harmony with it. The citizens are simply better informed and in direct control of their government.

Obviously, security would be the most important concern. Servers would have to be protected like military secrets and redundancies would have to be established to prevent tampering. The system must be trustworthy.

Once operational and utilized by a majority of the public, the system will generate an Open-Source Public Consensus of Policy. Society will collectively learn what works and what does not and our goal of Liberty and Justice for All will be closer to being realized than ever before.

Conspiracy and trolling are no longer widespread problems because they are inherently limited by their inability to inform consensus.

*Rabbit Hole Read! *See appendix c "LaB"*

Revolution in 3 easy steps:

Step 3 – Open Source Democracy

Once the systems of gathering and sharing quality data are in place, the process becomes almost fully automated. The new system is pouring out a recommended course of action on any policy topic. The system itself is constantly refined by consensus. In this new system, public policy will be dictated by the 'hive-mind' of all the citizens who wish to participate.

Now it is time to go to the ballot box and vote for

candidates who promise to implement the recommended policy. Once elected, if the official does not follow through on enacting the policies, we vote them out based on very clear parameters.

The art of bullshitting the public is no longer an accepted practice. We no longer need polarizing political parties, think tanks, and policy groups. The influence of money in our political system is gone. We have a virtual town square where bullshit goes to die. Lobbying is made to be ineffective and dies with the rest of the shadowy side of our government.

The integrity of the Democratic process increases

and progress is hastened. The efficiencies created in the government allow elected officials to keep their day jobs and not make a career out of politics.

It's an all-around cleaner running Democracy that allows us to trust and respect our government again.

As the world watches the United States continue to become *a more perfect union* there will be a sweeping global change.

It's time to be brave. It's time to be smart. It's time to reclaim our country and the values that it represents.

History will look back at us as the people who stood up for what is right.

Let's boot the snake oil salesmen out of our state institutions. Let's create a country and world that is better than when we found it.

Let's take the enormous pile of debt off of our grandchildren's backs and leave a healthy environment for them to enjoy.

Let's destroy the system that allows The Faction to exist and put layers of protection in place to prevent them from ever rising to power again.

Please understand that placing restrictions on the

accumulation of power is not punishing success. It is exactly what our country was founded on. We rejected the idea of kings from our very inception.

It is the combination of an ultra-wealthy Faction and the influence of money on politics that has created modern kings.

We can all agree that we don't want kings.

In the first Revolution we told a king to fuck off. This Revolution is only different in that we have multiple kings that need to fuck off.

That's it! Revolution in 3 easy steps!!!

No need for bloodshed. No need to alter the Constitution.

Our task is to allow the citizens to step into the role that the founders intended for them. **Educated and informed citizens are the most important branch of government.**

To summarize:

Step 1- Recognize that change is desperately needed, so start with yourself and open your mind.

Step 2- Continually watch out for ideas based on unbiased data that we can all agree on and then work outward from there.

Step 3- Let's create a system where experience and consensus dictate public policy and 'Liberty and Justice for All' is our guiding principle.

Let us whisper of this rebellion until the hearing aid of the empire is at full volume. Then, at that righteous time, we will challenge their power and our roar will deafen them as we approach! We are the New Patriots.

Section 3

Rabbit Hole Reads

Rabbit Hole Reads!

Additional fodder for your mind.

The following appendixes contain additional ideas and information you may find interesting.

One of the purposes of this book is to establish a means to bring these ideas to fruition.

Money definitely helps and is desperately needed but there are many ways you can help develop, refine, and manifest them.

Here are some of the other ways you can help:

-Share the book and its message.

-Offer your skills. We need help with graphic design, marketing, software development, accounting, and legal consultation... to name a few things. What do you do well?

-Send your ideas on how this book could be better!

-Share your ideas for a better world.

Appendix a -- Is this Liberty? Is this Justice?

-I believe that Individual Liberty reaches as far as another individual's Liberty. That is, if what I do doesn't affect anyone else's Liberty, then I should be free to do it. Live and Let Live.

-Until there is an injured party, there should be no law restricting an activity.

-If there is an injured party an impartial judgement of Justice should take place.

-I believe that Justice is the impartial cultivation and maintenance of fairness.

-Making things illegal does not prevent them from occurring. It only stresses the Justice system with unnecessary burdens. The Faction and Middle Management exploit this and their white collar crimes go unpunished. Beyond that, they make sure their favored method of corruption isn't illegal in the first place.

If we want Justice For All we need Liberty For All, if we want Liberty For All, we need Justice For All.

The one, likely necessary, exception is regulation. Regulations declare that if you are going to do this, then you must do that. If you are going to drive a car down the road, then you must wear a seatbelt. If you are going to drive a big truck, then you must pass through the weigh station. If you are going to operate a coal plant, you must properly dispose of your waste. Regulations live outside the scope of individual Liberty because they apply to everyone who performs a specific task and serve a major service to society as a whole.

-Who decides what needs regulated?

-A consensus should decide.

-Maybe there shouldn't be a seatbelt regulation.

-Maybe drugs shouldn't be illegal.

Only a majority consensus should decide this based on facts and data. It is not for The Faction to decide, they want no regulation for themselves and multitudes for the rest of us.

Appendix b – Dollar Trax

A completely transparent public accounting system. Dollar Trax can be used with tax or donation systems allowing public access to the revenue and spending of government or any organization's accounting ledger.

A completely transparent public accounting system.
Dollar Trax can be used with tax or donation
systems allowing public access to the revenue and
spending of government or any organization's
accounting ledger.

Complicated accounting is the tool of thieves.

Appendix c – LaB *(pronounced lah-bee or lobby...hehe)*

A social network designed to give all citizens equal access to government. Laws, policies, and regulations are debated in a secure, open forum with the goal of majority consensus dictating public policy.

Citizen's Civic Forum

A social network designed to give all citizens equal access to government. Laws, policies, and regulations are debated in a secure, open forum with the goal of a majority consensus dictating public policy.

Appendix d --- A Message from The New Patriots

Here is an excerpt from the novel *The New Patriot Rebellion*. It is an open letter from the New Patriots warning of the coming revolution:

Fellow Citizens,

We are witnessing the systematic takeover of the U.S. Government by a powerful faction. We can't see all the hands involved but we can see the results of their work. For some time, a force has been at work systematically dividing our country and moving to conquer it from within. The tenets of the modern national political parties work contrary to the intention of the framers of the U.S. Constitution. These national political parties, whatever their general intentions, have been used to weaken and conquer our country. The proof of this is built into their rallying cry, voiced in their intentions, and confirmed by their acts. This is a familiar foe as it is built into our own human nature and we must act swiftly and decisively to counter its power or we will continue to forge our own shackles.

A man in chains has been forced to believe he can't be free. A free man must believe, to that same degree, that he mustn't ever be chained.

The founders of our country made a colossal attempt to build safeguards into our system of government to prevent human nature from overpowering the basic protections of the individual. The concept of "Individual Liberty" was made the centerpiece of the founding documents. The United States Constitution is a functional work of art, a framework of protections against our very own nature and we must look to it in these dark times. With honest, best intention, the founders debated the wording of the concepts outlined in the Constitution. When one looks to the peripheral writings including the Federalist Papers and the other works of that time period, we see how the concepts took shape. Virtuous interpretation of the language and open consideration of the intention of these documents provide for a clear path forward.

There will be some who will reject this conclusion as they benefit too much from their own self-serving interpretation. They will vigorously defend their right to prosper at the expense of those that they oppress. They will not go quietly, they will seek to destroy those who speak out. The Second American Revolution is upon us but we hold an option for revolt that sheds no blood. It is our hope that this writing helps that cause.

A call to action, by pleasure or pain, must be followed by careful consideration of the steps to its resolve. A swift reaction, whether rabid lust or rampant rage, will surely offer no worthy resolution.

A faction of people have grown so intoxicated by greed and power that they are blind to the dire importance of their patriotism. They have worked to divide us and impose measures that further their personal interests. These citizens' illness mixed with public complacency and loose conspiracy brought us to this moment in time. Those who have distorted our system for their own gain are not acting wisely, in fact they act in blind fear of losing their power. The people who perpetuate the evil of oppressing other people do so at their own peril. They are blind to this reality. As they win in the name of their cause, we all lose

Independence and Liberty. Our collective complacency and the noise of conspiracy are equally to blame as we stand silent or ramble to no effect while these oppressors pillage and loot. We were very specifically warned of this menace by our founders' words and intent. History also shares vast experience of this force.

When it comes to the U.S. Constitution, in some areas, there are perpetual debates on what the founders' intentions were, but when one looks honestly, with virtue in their heart, at the periphery and considers the discussions the founders had while assembling the documents, their intention is very clear.

Individual Liberty is the delicate prize the founders sought to protect, this truth is impossible to deny.

In regards to illustrating the ills of our current situation, the writing that is perhaps the most compelling is George Washington's Farewell Address. It is powerful because it came at a time after our new country had operated according to the Constitution and he had experience to speak from. He saw where we were headed and gave us some insight of what was to come. The warnings contained in this address collectively illuminate the force behind the corruption that has come to be a part of our current system. At this time we must heed the words of our first president and hold close his parting gift.

Nothing could be more comforting than standing with the Father of Our Country to defeat the enemy of his work.

For this revolution, we will define our enemies by their

opposition to wise, virtuous, and immediate change. They will argue that the current political system is imperfect, yet generally good, and that it works to the benefit of all citizens. Do not be lured to this hope, the current political system does no such thing. They will use their positions of influence to block our advances. They will fail to apply the warnings in Washington's Farewell Address to the current evils they've built into the political system.

The enemy of Liberty will want to work through the current political parties for change but experience has shown this to be folly. We must reject all objections to our cause and find comfort in the words of the Father of Our Country, as his cause is our cause. We must embrace his Farewell Address and use it as a guide to defeat the subject of its warnings.

We must reject any voice of the current political parties as they are all tainted, at least in part, by the current corrupt system. We must make peace with the idea that any thought in harmony with the founders' intent and in chorus with this new movement will be voiced in multitude by the awakened souls of **The New Patriot Rebellion**.

You will know it is truly the voice of this Rebellion if it rings with the song of individual liberty, if it has wise dedication to peace on earth, and holds an unwavering flat rejection of the perpetrators behind the current corrupted system.

Be leery of those who claim special standing in this movement as the original architects have long since past. We have discovered this torch already burning, nearly snuffed out but its flame we intend to return to its full glory.

Our country has been infiltrated by the enemy of Liberty, an enemy that acts only for its own self-interest rather than doing virtuous work for the whole. The enemy has invaded our homes and poisoned our relationships... the enemy is the worst of our own human nature. We have allowed greed and corruption to take over and force their influence on us. Our enemy is within us, it has poisoned our minds to be less than decent, to cast judgement, and subsequently to divide us and cast us all into that same old slavery.

The Second American Revolution is upon us, we did not seek it, but our complacency and conspiracy invited it.

-True patriotism is working towards the best for every Citizen.

-True Patriotism is the work of strengthening the framework that offered you opportunity.

-True Patriotism is resisting the urge to use advantage to direct more power to yourself even though it is within your power to do so.

We have allowed a monster to take control,

x

x

overcoming it will not be easy, but we have no other choice. We either swallow the keys to our shackles in silence or rebel now.

Join us in defending our country against the tyranny imposed by the current government. Let us embrace the intentions of the founders and take back our Constitutionally protected right to Liberty For All.

 -The New Patriots

We open our eyes to see a sun obstructed in half by the horizon of earth and wonder whether it is rising or setting. But coming from such darkness, we know it surely must be rising.

Appendix e - George Washington's Farewell Address

Here is a paraphrased version of George Washington's Farewell Address along with the original text. There are 50 paragraphs. Paraphrasing in bold.

Friends and Citizens:

(1)   I do not wish to seek a third term as President.

(1)The period for a new election of a citizen to administer the executive government of the United States being not far distant,

and the time actually arrived
when your thoughts must be
employed in designating the
person who is to be clothed
with that important trust, it
appears to me proper,
especially as it may conduce
to a more distinct expression
of the public voice, that I
should now apprise you of the
resolution I have formed, to
decline being considered
among the number of those
out of whom a choice is to be
made.

(2) **Please know
that I have thought this
through and don't think
that because I'm leaving
my attitude has changed, I
still care deeply about the
future of the country and I**

**think it's going to be in
safe hands.**

(2)I beg you, at the same
time, to do me the justice to
be assured that this resolution
has not been taken without a
strict regard to all the
considerations appertaining to
the relation which binds a
dutiful citizen to his country;
and that in withdrawing the
tender of service, which
silence in my situation might
imply, I am influenced by no
diminution of zeal for your
future interest, no deficiency
of grateful respect for your
past kindness, but am
supported by a full conviction
that the step is compatible
with both.

**(3)   I didn't really
want to run for the second**

term but I did so because I thought it would be best for the country.

(3)The acceptance of, and continuance hitherto in, the office to which your suffrages have twice called me have been a uniform sacrifice of inclination to the opinion of duty and to a deference for what appeared to be your desire. I constantly hoped that it would have been much earlier in my power, consistently with motives which I was not at liberty to disregard, to return to that retirement from which I had been reluctantly drawn. The strength of my inclination to do this, previous to the last election, had even led to the preparation of an address to declare it to you; but mature reflection on the then perplexed and critical posture of our affairs with foreign nations, and the unanimous advice of persons entitled to my confidence, impelled me to abandon the idea.

(4)   I hope we can all agree that this is a good time for me to retire.

(4)I rejoice that the state of your concerns, external as well as internal, no longer renders the pursuit of inclination incompatible with the sentiment of duty or propriety, and am persuaded, whatever partiality may be retained for my services, that, in the present circumstances of our country, you will not disapprove my determination to retire.

(5) **I played an important role in getting this started but I'm getting old and the country must go on without me.**

(5)The impressions with which I first undertook the arduous trust were explained on the proper occasion. In the discharge of this trust, I will only say that I have, with good intentions, contributed towards the organization and administration of the government the best exertions of which a very fallible judgment was capable. Not unconscious in the outset of the inferiority of my qualifications, experience in my own eyes, perhaps still more in the eyes of others, has strengthened the motives to diffidence of myself; and every day the increasing weight of years admonishes me more and more that the shade of retirement is as necessary to me as it will be welcome. Satisfied that if any circumstances have given peculiar value to my services, they were temporary, I have the consolation to believe that, while choice and prudence invite me to quit the political scene, patriotism does not forbid it.

(6)   I am grateful for the opportunity. I did my best and tried very hard, but this job would have been impossible to

do without your support. I hope that the good work that we have done together goes on indefinitely and that it is a great example of Liberty to the rest of the world.

(6)In looking forward to the moment which is intended to terminate the career of my public life, my feelings do not permit me to suspend the deep acknowledgment of that debt of gratitude which I owe to my beloved country for the many honors it has conferred upon me; still more for the steadfast confidence with which it has supported me; and for the opportunities I have thence enjoyed of manifesting my inviolable attachment, by services faithful and persevering, though in usefulness unequal to my zeal. If benefits have resulted to our country from these services, let it always be remembered to your praise, and as an instructive example in our annals, that under circumstances in which the passions, agitated in every direction, were liable to mislead, amidst appearances sometimes dubious, vicissitudes of fortune often discouraging, in situations in which not unfrequently want of success has countenanced the spirit of criticism, the constancy of your support was the essential prop of the efforts, and a guarantee of the plans by which they were effected. Profoundly penetrated with this idea, I shall carry it with me to my grave, as a strong incitement to unceasing vows that heaven may continue to you the choicest tokens of its beneficence; that your union and brotherly affection may be perpetual; that the free Constitution, which is the work of your hands, may be sacredly maintained; that its administration in every department may be stamped with wisdom and virtue; that, in fine, the happiness of the people of these States, under the auspices of liberty, may be made complete by so careful a preservation and so prudent a use of this blessing as will acquire to them the glory of recommending it to the applause, the affection, and adoption of every nation which is yet a stranger to it

(7).   **This is probably where I should stop but I have some concerns I'd like to share. I wish to share some ideas that might help you after I'm gone. From my experience, observations, and careful consideration I can see serious threats to the work we have done. You can trust me because I have nothing to gain. Furthermore, you have always seemed to encourage and trust my opinions.**

(7)Here, perhaps, I ought to stop. But a solicitude for your welfare, which cannot end but with my life, and the apprehension of danger, natural to that solicitude, urge me, on an occasion like the present, to offer to your solemn contemplation, and to recommend to your frequent review, some sentiments which are the result of much reflection, of no inconsiderable observation, and which appear to me all-important to the permanency of your felicity as a people. These will be offered to you with the more freedom, as you can only see in them the disinterested warnings of a parting friend, who can possibly have no personal motive to bias his counsel. Nor can I forget, as an encouragement to it, your indulgent reception of my sentiments on a former and not dissimilar occasion.

(8).   **Your dedication to Liberty is not in question and you don't need me to confirm that.**

(8)Interwoven as is the love of liberty with every ligament of your hearts, no recommendation of mine is necessary to fortify or confirm the attachment.

(9).   **Having pride in your government is the most important contribution you can make to preserve all that you love; safety, independence, prosperity, and Liberty. We have to assume that there will be** forces at work that will try to sway your mind from this truth and to weaken your dedication to it. You must realize how important it is to value the unity of our nation. Your immovable attachment to the value of national unity is your protection against the loss of your safety, independence, prosperity, and Liberty.

(9)The unity of government which constitutes you one people is also now dear to you. It is justly so, for it is a main pillar in the edifice of your real independence, the support of your tranquility at home, your peace abroad; of your safety; of your prosperity; of that very liberty which you so highly prize. But as it is easy to foresee that, from different causes and from different quarters, much pains will be taken, many artifices employed to weaken in your minds the conviction of this truth; as this is the point in your political fortress against which the batteries of internal and external enemies will be most constantly and actively (though often covertly and insidiously) directed, it is of infinite moment that you should properly estimate the immense value of your national union to your collective and individual happiness; that you should cherish a cordial, habitual, and immovable attachment to it; accustoming yourselves to think and speak of it as of the palladium of your political safety and prosperity; watching for its preservation with jealous anxiety; discountenancing whatever may suggest even a suspicion that it can in any event be abandoned; and indignantly frowning upon the first dawning of every attempt to alienate any portion of our country from the rest, or to enfeeble the sacred ties which now link together the various parts.

(10)   Patriotism is a very honorable thing. Being proud of your country should be considered more important than any other designation. Our collective love of freedom

and liberty brought us together in a united cause. We have a free country because we worked together to achieve that status.

(10)For this you have every inducement of sympathy and interest. Citizens, by birth or choice, of a common country, that country has a right to concentrate your affections. The name of American, which belongs to you in your national capacity, must always exalt the just pride of patriotism more than any appellation derived from local discriminations. With slight shades of difference, you have the same religion, manners, habits, and political principles. You have in a common cause fought and triumphed together; the independence and liberty you possess are the work of joint counsels, and joint efforts of common dangers, sufferings, and successes.

(11)   Everyone will have passions of a local nature. Some ideas will be more important to different people in different places but without the protections of a national identity, all our personal passions will be lost.

(11)But these considerations, however powerfully they address themselves to your sensibility, are greatly outweighed by those which apply more immediately to your interest. Here every portion of our country finds the most commanding motives for carefully guarding and preserving the union of the whole.

(12) **For example, businesses in one state, because of the protections of national unity, are able to trade safely and more efficiently with another state thus making both more prosperous. These advantages far outweigh the benefits of each state going it alone.**

(12)The North, in an unrestrained intercourse with

the South, protected by the equal laws of a common government, finds in the productions of the latter great additional resources of maritime and commercial enterprise and precious materials of manufacturing industry. The South, in the same intercourse, benefiting by the agency of the North, sees its agriculture grow and its commerce expand. Turning partly into its own channels the seamen of the North, it finds its particular navigation invigorated; and, while it contributes, in different ways, to nourish and increase the general mass of the national navigation, it looks forward to the protection of a maritime strength, to which itself is unequally adapted. The East, in a like intercourse with the

West, already finds, and in the progressive improvement of interior communications by land and water, will more and more find a valuable vent for the commodities which it brings from abroad, or manufactures at home. The West derives from the East supplies requisite to its growth and comfort, and, what is perhaps of still greater consequence, it must of necessity owe the secure enjoyment of indispensable outlets for its own productions to the weight, influence, and the future maritime strength of the Atlantic side of the Union, directed by an indissoluble community of interest as one nation. Any other tenure by which the West can hold this essential advantage, whether derived from its own separate strength, or from an apostate and unnatural connection with any foreign power, must be intrinsically precarious.

(13)   With a strong national unity, all the states are safer from interruption of their peace and are protected from foreign influence. Because of our national unity, we can have a smaller military. A large overgrown military establishment is a serious threat to Liberty.

(13)While, then, every part of our country thus feels an immediate and particular interest in union, all the parts combined cannot fail to find in the united mass of means and efforts greater strength, greater resource, proportionably greater security from external danger, a less frequent interruption of their peace by foreign nations; and, what is of inestimable value, they must derive from union an exemption from those broils and wars between themselves, which so frequently afflict neighboring countries not tied together by the same governments, which their own rival ships alone would be sufficient to produce, but which opposite foreign alliances, attachments, and intrigues would stimulate and embitter. Hence, likewise, they will avoid the necessity of those overgrown military establishments which, under any form of government, are inauspicious to liberty, and which are to be regarded as particularly hostile to republican liberty. In this sense it is that your union ought to be considered as a main prop of your liberty, and that the love of the one ought to endear to you the preservation of the other.

(14)   We surely see the value of a strong national unity but is it possible for humans to hold it together? Let experience solve it. Speculation in this case is criminal. We've created a system which we believe will provide a good chance for a lasting bond of freedom and

Liberty. Let us see what happens... and those who speculate of failure or work to weaken it should not be trusted.

(14)These considerations speak a persuasive language to every reflecting and virtuous mind, and exhibit the continuance of the Union as a primary object of patriotic desire. Is there a doubt whether a common government can embrace so large a sphere? Let experience solve it. To listen to mere speculation in such a case were criminal. We are authorized to hope that a proper organization of the whole with the auxiliary agency of governments for the respective subdivisions, will afford a happy issue to the experiment. It is well worth a fair and full experiment. With such powerful and obvious motives to union, affecting all parts of our country, while experience shall not have demonstrated its impracticability, there will always be reason to distrust the patriotism of those who in any quarter may endeavor to weaken its bands.

(15)   When I try to imagine what might happen to destroy what we have created, I see regional political parties as a serious concern. In their zeal to win influence over another political party, there is a tendency of one

political party to misrepresent the goals of another. This is a very serious threat to our Liberty. Recently for example, our government was procuring a treaty with Spain. It was negotiated by the executive and ratified by the senate according to the design of our government and still those in the West speculated publicly that this was separately not in their best interest but instead favored other parts of the country. Time has shown their speculation to be false. Isn't it in their best interest to part of a unified nation, having a government working as designed, procuring an international agreement for the benefit of the union as a whole? Will they keep listening to the voices that seek to show divide between their own interest and the best interest of the entire union or seek to have a separate agreement with foreign nations?

(15)In contemplating the causes which may disturb our Union, it occurs as matter of serious concern that any ground should have been furnished for characterizing parties by geographical discriminations, Northern and Southern, Atlantic and Western; whence designing men may endeavor to excite a belief that there is a real difference of local interests and views. One of the expedients of party to acquire influence within particular districts is to misrepresent the opinions and aims of other districts. You cannot shield yourselves too much against the jealousies and heartburnings which spring from these misrepresentations; they tend to render alien to each other those who ought to be bound together by fraternal affection. The inhabitants of our Western country have lately had a useful lesson on this head; they have seen, in the negotiation by the Executive, and in the unanimous ratification by the Senate, of the treaty with Spain, and in the universal satisfaction at that event, throughout the United States, a decisive proof how unfounded were the suspicions propagated among them of a policy in the General Government and in the Atlantic States unfriendly to their interests in regard to the Mississippi; they have been witnesses to the formation of two treaties, that with Great Britain, and that with Spain, which secure to them everything they could desire, in respect to our foreign relations, towards confirming their prosperity. Will it not be their wisdom to rely for the preservation of these advantages on the Union by which they were procured ? Will they not henceforth be deaf to those advisers, if such there are, who would sever them from their brethren and connect them with aliens?

(16)   For the United States to be an effective and permanent union, faith in a central government is the most important aspect. Experience has shown that all other forms of government have failed to provide adequate protection from infractions and interruptions. It is so important that... we even

started over once in the process of searching for a true protection of Liberty. We put a lot of thought into the structure of this government, guided by true observations and honest deliberations and it deserves your upmost respect. Because we built into this union, rules for amendment and had mature deliberation of its structure, you should have faith in its processes and respect its laws.

(16)To the efficacy and permanency of your Union, a government for the whole is indispensable. No alliance, however strict, between the parts can be an adequate substitute; they must inevitably experience the infractions and interruptions which all alliances in all times have experienced. Sensible of this momentous truth, you have improved upon your first essay, by the adoption of a constitution of government better calculated than your former for an intimate union, and for the efficacious management of your common concerns. This government, the offspring of our own choice, uninfluenced and unawed, adopted upon full investigation and mature deliberation, completely free in its principles, in the distribution of its powers, uniting security with energy, and containing within itself a provision for its own amendment, has a just claim to your confidence and your support. Respect for its authority, compliance with its laws, acquiescence in its measures, are duties enjoined by the fundamental maxims of true liberty. The basis of our political systems is the right of the people to make and to alter their constitutions of government. But the Constitution which at any time exists, till changed by an explicit and authentic act of the whole people, is sacredly obligatory upon all. The very idea of the power and the right of the people to establish government presupposes the duty of every individual to obey the established government.

(17)   If a political party works to block the execution of laws or tries to direct or control the action of constitutionally elected officials this goes against the whole concept of our nation. Political parties and lobbyists create factions that, as factions, act like factions. Factions only work against the protections of Liberty we have created.

(17)All obstructions to the execution of the laws, all combinations and associations, under whatever plausible character, with the real design to direct, control, counteract, or awe the regular deliberation and action of the constituted authorities, are destructive of this fundamental principle, and of fatal tendency. They serve to organize faction, to give it an artificial and extraordinary force; to put, in the place of the delegated will of the nation the will of a party, often a small but artful and enterprising minority of the community; and, according to the alternate triumphs of different parties, to make the public administration the mirror of the ill-concerted and incongruous projects of faction, rather than the organ of consistent and wholesome plans digested by common counsels and modified by mutual interests.

(18) Political parties may, from time to time, do something that is in the interest of the entire nation but are then likely to eventually become the potent engines of unprincipled men who will use them to destroy the very processes that brought them to power.

(18)However combinations or associations of the above description may now and then answer popular ends, they are likely, in the course of time and things, to become potent engines, by which cunning, ambitious, and unprincipled men will be enabled to subvert the power of the people and to usurp for themselves the reins of government, destroying afterwards the very engines which have lifted them to unjust dominion.

(19)   In the interest of maintaining the privileges afforded you by your government, it is important that you speak up against those who disrespect its authority. You should be leery of those who wish to change its fundamental principles no matter what they claim. They may act to amend the Constitution to weaken it because it cannot be directly overthrown. Whenever a

change is proposed, remember that processes over time should be used to make changes and experience is much more valuable than hypothesis and opinion. Managing a large country is a big job and having a vigorous government is indispensable. With powers properly distributed and adjusted, Liberty will find its surest guardian. A government too feeble to stand up to factions is a government in name only and cannot protect person or property.

(19)Towards the preservation of your government, and the permanency of your present happy state, it is requisite, not only that you steadily discountenance irregular oppositions to its acknowledged authority, but also that you resist with care the spirit of innovation upon its principles, however specious the pretexts. One method of assault may be to effect, in the forms of the Constitution, alterations which will impair the energy of the system, and thus to undermine what cannot be directly overthrown. In all the changes to which you may be invited, remember that time and habit are at least as necessary to fix the true character of governments as of other human institutions; that experience is the surest standard by which to test the real tendency of the existing constitution of a country; that facility in changes, upon the credit of mere hypothesis and opinion, exposes to perpetual change, from the endless variety of hypothesis and opinion; and remember, especially, that for the efficient management of your common interests, in a country so extensive as ours, a government of as much vigor as is consistent with the perfect security of liberty is indispensable. Liberty itself will find in such a government, with powers properly distributed and adjusted, its surest guardian. It is, indeed, little else than a name, where the government is too feeble to withstand the enterprises of faction, to confine each member of the society within the limits prescribed by the laws, and to maintain all in the secure and tranquil enjoyment of the rights of person and property.

(20)   I've already commented on the dangers of political parties in regards to geography. Now I will comment on political parties and lobbyists in general.

(20)I have already intimated to you the danger of parties in the State, with particular reference to the founding of them on geographical discriminations. Let me now take a more comprehensive view, and warn you in the most solemn manner against the baneful effects of the spirit of party generally.

(21)   The spirit of political parties is rooted in human nature and exists in all forms of government. But in popular governments, it is truly their worst enemy.

(21)This spirit, unfortunately, is inseparable from our nature, having its root in the strongest passions of the human mind. It exists under different shapes in all governments, more or less stifled, controlled, or repressed; but, in those of the popular form, it is seen in its greatest rankness, and is truly their worst enemy.

(22)   The alternating exchange of power of one political party over another, sharpened by the spirit of revenge, which history has shown to perpetuate grand atrocities, becomes itself a new kind of despotism. The disorder created by this vengeful back and forth creates the environment where men might see security in the absolute power of an individual. Eventually the leader of one of the political parties by his

**abilities or fortune, will
take over and stand on
the ruins of public Liberty.**

(22)The alternate
domination of one faction over
another, sharpened by the
spirit of revenge, natural to
party dissension, which in
different ages and countries
has perpetrated the most
horrid enormities, is itself a
frightful despotism. But this
leads at length to a more
formal and permanent
despotism. The disorders and
miseries which result
gradually incline the minds of
men to seek security and
repose in the absolute power
of an individual; and sooner or
later the chief of some
prevailing faction, more able
or more fortunate than his

competitors, turns this disposition to the purposes of his own elevation, on the ruins of public liberty.

(23) **This example may sound extreme but wise people should not underestimate the common and continual mischiefs of political parties and lobbyists and should discourage and restrain them.**

(23)Without looking forward to an extremity of this kind (which nevertheless ought not to be entirely out of sight), the common and continual mischiefs of the spirit of party are sufficient to make it the interest and duty of a wise people to discourage and restrain it.

(24)   Political parties and lobbyists distract the public and work to weaken the public administration. They agitate the community with unfounded jealousies and create false alarms. They bring animosity over one against another. It opens the door to foreign influence, which finds easier access to the government through the channels of party passions... making the policy of one country

subject to the policies and will of another.

(24)It serves always to distract the public councils and enfeeble the public administration. It agitates the community with ill-founded jealousies and false alarms, kindles the animosity of one part against another, foments occasionally riot and insurrection. It opens the door to foreign influence and corruption, which finds a facilitated access to the government itself through the channels of party passions. Thus the policy and the will of one country are subjected to the policy and will of another.

(25)   Some say that political parties are a good

**check against the
administration of
government. The value of
any good they do is
outweighed by the danger
of their excess.**

(25)There is an opinion that
parties in free countries are
useful checks upon the
administration of the
government and serve to
keep alive the spirit of liberty.
This within certain limits is
probably true; and in
governments of a monarchical
cast, patriotism may look with
indulgence, if not with favor,
upon the spirit of party. But in
those of the popular
character, in governments
purely elective, it is a spirit not
to be encouraged. From their
natural tendency, it is certain

there will always be enough of that spirit for every salutary purpose. And there being constant danger of excess, the effort ought to be by force of public opinion, to mitigate and assuage it. A fire not to be quenched, it demands a uniform vigilance to prevent its bursting into a flame, lest, instead of warming, it should consume.

(26)   **Knowledgeable and free thinking citizens are a safety check against the consolidation of power between the branches of government. If a problem arises, it should be dealt with by amendment to the Constitution. Even if a modification is made**

outside the Constitutional framework for the good of Liberty it still opens the door to the destruction of our free government.

(26)It is important, likewise, that the habits of thinking in a free country should inspire caution in those entrusted with its administration, to confine themselves within their respective constitutional spheres, avoiding in the exercise of the powers of one department to encroach upon another. The spirit of encroachment tends to consolidate the powers of all the departments in one, and thus to create, whatever the form of government, a real despotism. A just estimate of that love of power, and proneness to abuse it, which predominates in the human heart, is sufficient to satisfy us of the truth of this position. The necessity of reciprocal checks in the exercise of political power, by dividing and distributing it into different depositaries, and constituting each the guardian of the public weal against invasions by the others, has been evinced by experiments ancient and modern; some of them in our country and under our own eyes. To preserve them must be as necessary as to institute them. If, in the opinion of the people, the distribution or modification of the constitutional powers be in any particular wrong, let it be corrected by an amendment in the way which the Constitution designates.

But let there be no change by usurpation; for though this, in one instance, may be the instrument of good, it is the customary weapon by which free governments are destroyed. The precedent must always greatly overbalance in permanent evil any partial or transient benefit, which the use can at any time yield.

(27)   Religion and morality are important supports of our Constitutional government. You cannot be a true patriot and ignore this. Can you trust the oaths of office and of the courts without the moral obligation that religion provides? If we

cautiously consider that morality can exist without religion, reason and experience, thus far, have shown this not to be true.

(27)Of all the dispositions and habits which lead to political prosperity, religion and morality are indispensable supports. In vain would that man claim the tribute of patriotism, who should labor to subvert these great pillars of human happiness, these firmest props of the duties of men and citizens. The mere politician, equally with the pious man, ought to respect and to cherish them. A volume could not trace all their connections with private and public felicity. Let it simply be asked: Where is the security for property, for reputation, for life, if the sense of religious obligation desert the oaths which are the instruments of investigation in courts of justice ? And let us with caution indulge the supposition that morality can be maintained without religion. Whatever may be conceded to the influence of refined education on minds of peculiar structure, reason and experience both forbid us to expect that national morality can prevail in exclusion of religious principle.

(28)   **Virtue and morality are necessary to a popular government. What is the point of arguing against this?**

(28)It is substantially true that virtue or morality is a necessary spring of popular government. The rule, indeed, extends with more or less force to every species of free government. Who that is a sincere friend to it can look with indifference upon attempts to shake the foundation of the fabric?

> (29)   **It is of the upmost importance to have an educated public. As the structure of government is shaped by public opinion, it is important that the public be equally educated to that end.**

(29)Promote then, as an object of primary importance, institutions for the general diffusion of knowledge. In proportion as the structure of a government gives force to public opinion, it is essential that public opinion should be enlightened.

(30)   As an important source of strength and security, we must keep public credit sacred. The best way to keep it sacred is to use it sparingly. War is expensive so cultivating peace saves money. After a war, we should pay back our bills as fast as possible as to not pass them on to future generations. The public should pressure the representatives to do this. The public should also

keep in mind that paying debts requires revenue and revenue requires taxes, and no taxes are pleasant. The public should keep that in mind when they support representatives and government actions.

(30)As a very important source of strength and security, cherish public credit. One method of preserving it is to use it as sparingly as possible, avoiding occasions of expense by cultivating peace, but remembering also that timely disbursements to prepare for danger frequently prevent much greater disbursements to repel it, avoiding likewise the accumulation of debt, not only by shunning occasions of expense, but by vigorous exertion in time of peace to discharge the debts which unavoidable wars may have occasioned, not ungenerously throwing upon posterity the burden which we ourselves ought to bear. The execution of these maxims belongs to your representatives, but it is necessary that public opinion should co-operate. To facilitate to them the performance of their duty, it is essential that you should practically bear in mind that towards the payment of debts there must be revenue; that to have revenue there must be taxes; that no taxes can be devised which are not more or less inconvenient and unpleasant; that the intrinsic embarrassment, inseparable from the selection of the proper objects (which is always a choice of difficulties), ought to be a decisive motive for a candid construction of the conduct of the government in making it, and for a spirit of acquiescence in the measures for obtaining revenue, which the public exigencies may at any time dictate.

(31) We should wish the best for all nations and cultivate peace and harmony with all. As a nation with religion and morality as our guiding principles, we can be an example to the world. We should find that peace and

harmony is also a financially responsible policy. Wouldn't God favor a nation who works toward peace and harmony? It seems to be very much worth a try. In the end will we let it be defeated by bad habits?

(31)Observe good faith and justice towards all nations; cultivate peace and harmony with all. Religion and morality enjoin this conduct; and can it be, that good policy does not equally enjoin it - It will be worthy of a free, enlightened, and at no distant period, a great nation, to give to mankind the magnanimous and too novel example of a people always guided by an exalted justice and benevolence. Who can doubt that, in the course of time and things, the fruits of such a plan would richly repay any temporary advantages which might be lost by a steady adherence to it ? Can it be that Providence has not connected the permanent felicity of a nation with its virtue ? The experiment, at least, is recommended by every sentiment which ennobles human nature. Alas! is it rendered impossible by its vices?

(32)   As we try to maintain peace and harmony with all nations, we should not be overly fond or overly adversarial to any nation. Either of these makes us a

slave to them. In one case you become a slave to the animosity, the other, a slave to affection. Our country would then be weakened by the urge to act too early or too harsh, or too late or too light. We might let passions ignite actions that reason would reject.

(32)In the execution of such a plan, nothing is more essential than that permanent, inveterate antipathies against particular nations, and passionate attachments for others, should be excluded; and that, in place of them, just and amicable feelings towards all should be cultivated. The nation which indulges towards another a habitual hatred or a habitual fondness is in some degree a slave. It is a slave to its animosity or to its affection, either of which is sufficient to lead it astray from its duty and its interest. Antipathy in one nation against another disposes each more readily to offer insult and injury, to lay hold of slight causes of umbrage, and to be haughty and intractable, when accidental or trifling occasions of dispute occur. Hence, frequent collisions, obstinate, envenomed, and bloody contests. The nation, prompted by ill-will and resentment, sometimes impels to war the government, contrary to the best calculations of policy. The government sometimes participates in the national propensity, and adopts through passion what reason would reject; at other times it makes the animosity of the nation subservient to projects of hostility instigated by pride, ambition, and other sinister and pernicious motives. The peace often, sometimes perhaps the liberty, of nations, has been the victim.

(33)   **Favoritism towards a foreign nation produces additional evils. We could be pulled into conflicts with less than adequate justification, we might grant exceptions that are not in our best interest. Favoring one nation over another may prevent agreements that are in the**

best interest of our nation. Citizens may be inspired to betray or sacrifice their own country in a sense of obligation, ambition, or infatuation.

(33)So likewise, a passionate attachment of one nation for another produces a variety of evils. Sympathy for the favorite nation, facilitating the illusion of an imaginary common interest in cases where no real common interest exists, and infusing into one the enmities of the other, betrays the former into a participation in the quarrels and wars of the latter without adequate inducement or justification. It leads also to concessions to the favorite nation of privileges denied to others which is apt doubly to injure the nation making the concessions; by unnecessarily parting with what ought to have been retained, and by exciting jealousy, ill-will, and a disposition to retaliate, in the parties from whom equal privileges are withheld. And it gives to ambitious, corrupted, or deluded citizens (who devote themselves to the favorite nation), facility to betray or sacrifice the interests of their own country, without odium, sometimes even with popularity; gilding, with the appearances of a virtuous sense of obligation, a commendable deference for public opinion, or a laudable zeal for public good, the base or foolish compliances of ambition, corruption, or infatuation.

(34)   A truly enlightened and independent patriot will no doubt see the danger of foreign influence. A favored foreign influence may influence domestic factions, seduce the weak of mind, mislead public opinion, or influence public administrations. Such an attachment of a small or weak towards a great and powerful nation dooms the former to be the satellite of the latter

(34)As avenues to foreign influence in innumerable

ways, such attachments are particularly alarming to the truly enlightened and independent patriot. How many opportunities do they afford to tamper with domestic factions, to practice the arts of seduction, to mislead public opinion, to influence or awe the public councils. Such an attachment of a small or weak towards a great and powerful nation dooms the former to be the satellite of the latter.

(35)   Foreign influence is one of the worst threats to our Republic. Excessive favoritism or animosity makes one blind to dangers that impartiality would have seen. In either case, a real Patriot might

**be held suspect for
disagreeing and thus a
true protector of Liberty is
cast aside and the public
may be duped into
surrendering their
interests.**

(35)Against the insidious
wiles of foreign influence (I
conjure you to believe me,
fellow-citizens) the jealousy of
a free people ought to be
constantly awake, since
history and experience prove
that foreign influence is one of
the most baneful foes of
republican government. But
that jealousy to be useful
must be impartial; else it
becomes the instrument of the
very influence to be avoided,
instead of a defense against
it. Excessive partiality for one

foreign nation and excessive dislike of another cause those whom they actuate to see danger only on one side, and serve to veil and even second the arts of influence on the other. Real patriots who may resist the intrigues of the favorite are liable to become suspected and odious, while its tools and dupes usurp the applause and confidence of the people, to surrender their interests.

(36)   We should have trade with foreign nations but it should be absolutely separate of political connection. Other countries have varying priorities and we should

**remain independent of
their controversies.**

(36)The great rule of conduct for us in regard to foreign nations is in extending our commercial relations, to have with them as little political connection as possible. So far as we have already formed engagements, let them be fulfilled with perfect good faith. Here let us stop. Europe has a set of primary interests which to us have none; or a very remote relation. Hence she must be engaged in frequent controversies, the causes of which are essentially foreign to our concerns. Hence, therefore, it must be unwise in us to implicate ourselves by artificial ties in the ordinary vicissitudes of her politics, or the ordinary combinations and collisions of her friendships or enmities.

(37)   If we stay out of other nations controversies it enables us to choose a course of our own design. We may choose to cut ties with nations who get belligerent without fear of any loss besides basic trade. We are able to make strategic decisions without influence or fear. We are less likely to be provoked because we are never weakened by animosity or admiration. We are free to choose war

or peace without influence.

(37)Our detached and distant situation invites and enables us to pursue a different course. If we remain one people under an efficient government. the period is not far off when we may defy material injury from external annoyance; when we may take such an attitude as will cause the neutrality we may at any time resolve upon to be scrupulously respected; when belligerent nations, under the impossibility of making acquisitions upon us, will not lightly hazard the giving us provocation; when we may choose peace or war, as our interest, guided by justice, shall counsel.

(38)   Why would we give up the advantage of being fluid and able to adapt our position for the good of our nation? Why give any part of our independence away for opportunity on foreign soil? We have full control of our destiny, why give any part of that up?

(38)Why forego the advantages of so peculiar a situation? Why quit our own to stand upon foreign ground? Why, by interweaving our destiny with that of any part of Europe, entangle our peace and prosperity in the toils of European ambition, rivalship, interest, humor or caprice?

(39) It's a possibility that
there may be times when
engagement with foreign
nations might be
necessary. If this is so,
whether public or private,
let honesty be the best
policy. If you are going to
have an agreement with a
foreign entity, let your
interactions be observed
in a transparent, honest
way. But, I think it is
unwise to have
agreements with foreign
nations.

(39)It is our true policy to
steer clear of permanent
alliances with any portion of
the foreign world; so far, I
mean, as we are now at

liberty to do it; for let me not be understood as capable of patronizing infidelity to existing engagements. I hold the maxim no less applicable to public than to private affairs, that honesty is always the best policy. I repeat it, therefore, let those engagements be observed in their genuine sense. But, in my opinion, it is unnecessary and would be unwise to extend them.

(40)   In the case of defense, having foreign impartiality leaves us options and flexibility to make short term alliances for emergencies.

(40)Taking care always to keep ourselves by suitable

establishments on a respectable defensive posture, we may safely trust to temporary alliances for extraordinary emergencies.

(41)   Having peace and harmony with all nations is good policy, good for humanity, good financially. Commercial policy should take the same approach. Let markets develop naturally, without influencing rules to your advantage. *When legal advantages for U.S. companies are created in a foreign nation, they are paying for it with our independence.* **This policy**

of giving 'favors' in exchange for something generally ends with someone who believes they didn't get an equal value in the exchange. Experience has taught us that this has no way of ending well.

(41)Harmony, liberal intercourse with all nations, are recommended by policy, humanity, and interest. But even our commercial policy should hold an equal and impartial hand; neither seeking nor granting exclusive favors or preferences; consulting the natural course of things; diffusing and diversifying by gentle means the streams of commerce, but

forcing nothing; establishing
(with powers so disposed, in
order to give trade a stable
course, to define the rights of
our merchants, and to enable
the government to support
them) conventional rules of
intercourse, the best that
present circumstances and
mutual opinion will permit, but
temporary, and liable to be
from time to time abandoned
or varied, as experience and
circumstances shall dictate;
constantly keeping in view
that it is folly in one nation to
look for disinterested favors
from another; that it must pay
with a portion of its
independence for whatever it
may accept under that
character; that, by such
acceptance, it may place itself
in the condition of having
given equivalents for nominal

favors, and yet of being reproached with ingratitude for not giving more. There can be no greater error than to expect or calculate upon real favors from nation to nation. It is an illusion, which experience must cure, which a just pride ought to discard.

(42)   As I offer these words to you as an old friend, I must doubt they might make a strong and lasting impression, or that they might help to control the usual current of passions or prevent our country from going the way of every other country up until now. But if these words could be

productive in some way, perhaps they could be used to moderate the fury of political party spirit or to warn against the mischiefs of foreign intrigue. If these words could be a warning of imposters who pose as Patriots. This hope applies to all the ways your welfare may be threatened.

(42)In offering to you, my countrymen, these counsels of an old and affectionate friend, I dare not hope they will make the strong and lasting impression I could wish; that they will control the usual current of the passions, or prevent our nation from running the course which has hitherto marked the destiny of nations. But, if I may even flatter myself that they may be productive of some partial benefit, some occasional good; that they may now and then recur to moderate the fury of party spirit, to warn against the mischiefs of foreign intrigue, to guard against the impostures of pretended patriotism; this hope will be a full recompense for the solicitude for your welfare, by which they have been dictated.

(43)   The official historical records will tell how well I did my job. I know I did a good job.

(43)How far in the discharge of my official duties I have been guided by the principles which have been delineated, the public records and other evidences of my conduct must witness to you and to the world. To myself, the assurance of my own conscience is, that I have at least believed myself to be guided by them.

(44)   My opinion about the war in Europe has not changed. It was approved by both houses of congress and it is official policy.

(44)In relation to the still subsisting war in Europe, my proclamation of the twenty-second of April, 1793, is the index of my plan. Sanctioned by your approving voice, and by that of your representatives in both houses of Congress, the spirit of that measure has continually governed me, uninfluenced by any attempts to deter or divert me from it.

(45)   All things considered, we definitely should take a neutral position regarding the war in Europe. This was my position at the beginning and I adamantly still feel the same way.

(45)After deliberate examination, with the aid of the best lights I could obtain, I was well satisfied that our country, under all the circumstances of the case, had a right to take, and was bound in duty and interest to take, a neutral position. Having taken it, I determined, as far as should depend upon me, to maintain it, with moderation, perseverance, and firmness.

(46)   Last time I checked, making this decision was part of my job.

(46)The considerations which respect the right to hold this conduct, it is not necessary on this occasion to detail. I will only observe that, according to my understanding of the matter, that right, so far from being denied by any of the belligerent powers, has been virtually admitted by all.

(47)   We should always favor remaining neutral.

(47)The duty of holding a neutral conduct may be inferred, without anything more, from the obligation which justice and humanity impose on every nation, in cases in which it is free to act, to maintain inviolate the relations of peace and amity towards other nations.

(48)   We all have our own view of the matter but my primary motivation for remaining neutral was to give our country time to settle in. To give it time enough to be in command of its own fortunes.

(48)The inducements of interest for observing that conduct will best be referred to your own reflections and experience. With me a predominant motive has been to endeavor to gain time to our country to settle and mature its yet recent institutions, and to progress without interruption to that degree of strength and consistency which is necessary to give it, humanly speaking, the command of its own fortunes.

(49)   I may have made some errors but I know of none that were intentional. I hope that the greater good might see to it that my mistakes cause the least harm

possible. Please see my mistakes and learn from them, as I am retiring and can't make them right personally.

(49)Though, in reviewing the incidents of my administration, I am unconscious of intentional error, I am nevertheless too sensible of my defects not to think it probable that I may have committed many errors. Whatever they may be, I fervently beseech the Almighty to avert or mitigate the evils to which they may tend. I shall also carry with me the hope that my country will never cease to view them with indulgence; and that, after forty five years of my life dedicated to its service with an upright zeal, the faults of incompetent abilities will be consigned to oblivion, as myself must soon be to the mansions of rest.

(50)   I have seen and experienced myself, several generations of people living in a free land and I look forward to reliving the memories of working with everyone who helped create this. This is the reward of our mutual cares, labors, and dangers.

(50)Relying on its kindness in this as in other things, and actuated by that fervent love towards it, which is so natural to a man who views in it the native soil of himself and his progenitors for several generations, I anticipate with pleasing expectation that retreat in which I promise myself to realize, without alloy, the sweet enjoyment of partaking, in the midst of my fellow-citizens, the benign influence of good laws under a free government, the ever-favorite object of my heart, and the happy reward, as I trust, of our mutual cares, labors, and dangers.

-Geo. Washington.

Appendix f – Revolutionary Ideas

Water Battery- A single home or neighborhood water tower that fills by renewable means (solar, wind, batteries). Once the water is stored high off the ground, a small stream of falling water can turn a water wheel connected to gears and by mechanical advantage turn a flywheel. This produces continuous, secure electrical energy.

<u>Garbage Recipe-</u> A mix of bacteria, fungi, and other organisms that work in harmony to render household garbage back to organic matter. The right combination of organisms will render plastics and other pollutants back to good ol' dirt.

Henry George- A brilliant economist with ideas worth considering. His main point was that land speculation prevents people from accessing resources thereby hindering the advancement of society. Currently, a wealthy person buys up tracts of land and waits for profit while a person with a personal need or an idea for a business use of that land is unable to access it. This is an unjust system and prohibits progress. Henry George suggests a land rent system that encourages people to only hold land that they have a current use for and discourages land speculation. The implications are far reaching and ripple through society.

<u>Local Economies-</u> Developing local and regional economies creates massive efficiencies that lower costs and environmental impacts. Having a regional balance between the supply and demand of goods and services will make for an exceptionally stable economy. Quality is increased and quantity is relative to the region and overproduction is minimized.

This will work especially well in the food production system. Here's a fun list!

10 reasons why you should live within walking distance to 8 small sustainable farms...

1. FRESH FOOD TASTES BETTER. Grown for taste rather than shelf life, fresh local food has amazing flavors. As we returned to growing and canning our own tomatoes we were blown away by all the flavor we'd been missing when we purchased 'store bought' tomatoes. Being surrounded by small sustainable farms has another more important impact on your life. It makes your environment full of beautiful growth that attracts birds, produces flowers, and builds an economy based on agriculture and tourism rather than dirty factories.

2. FRESH FOOD IS HEALTHIER. The moment a vegetable is picked, in most cases, it starts to lose nutrients. The more food is processed, the more nutrients are lost. Fresh food does not require being sprayed to help preserve it for long truck drives.

3. YOU CAN'T EAT MONEY. Even if you have all the money in the world

you will starve if there is no one growing food. Since someone has to be growing the food, might as well be right down the road.

4. FOOD SECURITY. If anything bad should happen to our nation, we really, really hope it doesn't, be it economic or otherwise, your food source is very vulnerable if it comes from far away. It takes a few seasons of growing before you have the resources needed to sustainably farm so get started today!

5. LOCALIZED IMMUNITIES. It only makes sense that if you are eating the foods that are grown around you locally, it would help your body process the pollens and other allergens. It surely can't hurt....)

6. LOCAL ECONOMY. When you support local business your money isn't buying a 3rd house in France for some wealthy corporate person. Your money is way more likely to stay local

and be invested or spent locally....
making your life better!

7. HUMAN ERROR HAPPENS. When
the leadership of a large corporate
farm makes a mistake, you pay for it.
When one of your 8 local farmers
makes a mistake, you've got 7 more
to turn to. Diverse tactics allow
failure to be isolated and have less
impact on you.

8. CORPORATE FARMING CREATES
ITS OWN PROBLEMS. What do you do
when you have thousands of animals
in a small space? Well you have to
give them antibiotics so they don't
spread disease like the plague. You
have a real environmental problem
with so much waste in a small
space... its toxic pollution of the
highest order. There is security in
diversity... when you have a bunch of
the same thing in one small space,
the bugs and disease have an easy
go. When it comes to food

production, smaller is better, diverse is better, sustainable is better...

9. SUSTAINABLE FARMING IMPROVES THE SOIL EACH SEASON. Rather than using harsh chemicals, the sustainable farm builds nutrients and pest resistance by creating living soil with micro-organisms, beneficial fungi, earthworms, etc... Seasonal crop rotation keeps the pests guessing and moving so they make mistakes... getting eaten or lost before they find the wonderful buffet in its new place in the garden. Companion planting allows plants to work together to keep bad stuff away. Corporate farms simply kill off everything in the soil and add the nutrients they want, wasting vast amounts of gas and oil as well as putting harsh chemicals on your food. We have yet to find someone who enjoys the taste of harsh chemicals and we're pretty sure harsh chemicals are not the best thing to put into your body.

10. THERE IS NOT AN UNLIMITED SUPPLY OF OIL AND GAS. The earth will run out. But before that happens... unless you are very wealthy, you will be priced out of the game. Large corporate farms use vast amounts of oil and gas to acquire the fertilizers, plow large fields, transport the products, etc... The price you pay at the grocery store directly reflects the cost of oil and gas. As the supply of oil and gas gets smaller, the price will get higher. Corporate greed has blinded the folks who make our food and they are not changing anything. The corporate farm model will inevitably collapse because it is unsustainable without cheap oil and gas.

Bulk Services buying power-

Using the buying power of our entire country to leverage lower pricing on goods and services that we buy in bulk. This is the same idea employed by Home Depot, Best buy, Walmart, etc. There are some products and services that we should purchase as a group at a discounted rate.

Community Supported Production Efficiencies-

When a community invests in infrastructure there are efficiencies created in the private production market. For instance, if you have natural gas pipes running through a town, this encourages natural gas products to be purchased by the citizens. The producers of those natural gas products can utilize production efficiencies because of the increased volume of purchases created by the infrastructure investment. So when a community decides to invest in infrastructure, they are stimulating the related industries and costs will come down. Investment in systems that are overall better for the community but currently cost more should account for these efficiencies.

National Union- A national labor union for all U.S. workers that works to establish fair compensation and other basic protections. A forward thinking organization that anticipates trends and provides education opportunities. This will create an inherent flexibility in the workforce that allows workers to serve businesses better during peak production while keeping workers stabile during slow periods.

<u>Universal Consumer Rights</u>
<u>Declaration–</u> A declaration that
supersedes all fine print legal
jargon used by corporations. The
UCRD protects consumers from
unfair and deceptive language
built into service contracts and
'terms and conditions'. If
businesses are allowed to
include "fine print" legal
protections into their
transactions, the consumer
should be able to as well. When
signing a terms of service
agreement the consumer simply
adds "UCRD applies" to the end
of their signature.

The UCRD declares that:

"Using complex legal language
or any other tactic that is
misleading, whether intended or

not, in any contract or terms and conditions agreement is not legally binding and the contract is signed under duress."

Apprentice Education- Build a system of education based on skilled trades rather than singular academia. Apprenticeship programs to educate students in real world practices. As technology swallows up the jobs of past generations our current education system lacks the flexibility and diversity needed to adjust to the new economy.

Geothermal and other alternative infrastructure investment ideas- Invest in home efficiencies like furnaces (geothermal or high efficiency), appliances, windows and doors. Instead of building a new power plant, the energy producer invests in high efficiency products for citizen's homes. The citizen pays a similar bill as before the improvements but the savings incurred by the more efficient systems is used as a monthly payment for the new equipment.

<u>Human rights based trade policies-</u> This is simple. Countries must meet basic human rights standards in order to trade with the U.S. This will create a more just environment for U.S. companies and workers. Countries and companies who allow slave wage labor or poor conditions won't be able to trade with the U.S. and companies within the U.S. will not be able to sell their foreign made products in the U.S. unless they meet the basic human rights requirements.

Do you want to help develop these ideas?

Visit:

newpatriotrebellion.org

Email:

newpatriotrebel@gmail.com

May our children see a day when basic decency rules this land.